PIANO • VOCAL • GUITAR

The Essential GERSHWIN®

SHEET MUSIC COLLECTION

Produced by
Alfred Music Publishing Co., Inc.
P.O. Box 10003
Van Nuys, CA 91410-0003
alfred.com

Printed in USA.

ISBN-10: 0-7390-7022-3
ISBN-13: 978-0-7390-7022-2

Cover Photo:
© Mike Liu | Dreamstime.com

 Alfred Cares. Contents printed on 100% recycled paper.

CONTENTS

TITLE	SHOW / FILM	PAGE

An American in Paris .... AN AMERICAN IN PARIS 4

(I've Got) Beginner's Luck .... SHALL WE DANCE 12

Bess, You Is My Woman .... PORGY AND BESS 16

Bidin' My Time .... GIRL CRAZY 25

But Not for Me .... GIRL CRAZY 28

Embraceable You .... GIRL CRAZY 32

Fascinating Rhythm .... LADY, BE GOOD! 36

A Foggy Day (in London Town) .... A DAMSEL IN DISTRESS 40

For You, For Me, For Evermore .... THE SHOCKING MISS PILGRIM 44

How Long Has This Been Going On? .... ROSALIE 48

I Can't Be Bothered Now .... A DAMSEL IN DISTRESS 53

I Can't Get Started .... ZIEGFELD FOLLIES OF 1936 58

I Got Rhythm .... GIRL CRAZY 62

Isn't It a Pity? .... PARDON MY ENGLISH 72

It Ain't Necessarily So .... PORGY AND BESS 66

It's a New World .... A STAR IS BORN 77

I've Got a Crush on You .... TREASURE GIRL / STRIKE UP THE BAND 82

Let's Call the Whole Thing Off .... SHALL WE DANCE 86

Liza (All the Clouds'll Roll Away) .... SHOW GIRL 90

Long Ago (and Far Away) .... COVER GIRL 94

Love Is Here to Stay .... THE GOLDWYN FOLLIES 100

Love Is Sweeping the Country .... OF THEE I SING 120

Love Walked In .... THE GOLDWYN FOLLIES 104

CONTENTS

TITLE	SHOW / FILM	PAGE
The Man I Love	LADY, BE GOOD! / STRIKE UP THE BAND	116
The Man That Got Away	A STAR IS BORN	108
My Ship	LADY IN THE DARK	97
Nice Work if You Can Get It	A DAMSEL IN DISTRESS	124
Oh, Lady Be Good	LADY, BE GOOD!	113
Prelude I		128
Rhapsody in Blue		132
'S Wonderful	FUNNY FACE	140
Shall We Dance	SHALL WE DANCE	144
Slap That Bass	SHALL WE DANCE	148
Somebody Loves Me	GEORGE WHITE'S SCANDALS OF 1924	170
Someone to Watch Over Me	OH, KAY!	158
(I'll Build a) Stairway to Paradise	GEORGE WHITE'S SCANDALS OF 1922	162
Stiff Upper Lip	A DAMSEL IN DISTRESS	166
Strike Up the Band	STRIKE UP THE BAND	153
Summertime	PORGY AND BESS	174
Swanee	DEMI TASSE REVUE	182
Sweet and Low-Down	TIP-TOES	188
They All Laughed	SHALL WE DANCE	177
They Can't Take That Away from Me	SHALL WE DANCE	192
Things Are Looking Up	A DAMSEL IN DISTRESS	196
Tschaikowsky (and Other Russians)	LADY IN THE DARK	200
Who Cares?	OF THEE I SING	205

AN AMERICAN IN PARIS
(In Miniature)

By GEORGE GERSHWIN
Paraphrased and Arranged by
MAURICE C. WHITNEY

6

Blues tempo
Andante ma con ritmo deciso

10

(I'VE GOT) BEGINNER'S LUCK

(from *Shall We Dance*)

Music and Lyrics by
GEORGE GERSHWIN
and IRA GERSHWIN

(I've Got) Beginner's Luck - 4 - 1

BESS, YOU IS MY WOMAN

(from *Porgy and Bess*)

Music and Lyrics by
GEORGE GERSHWIN, IRA GERSHWIN
and DuBOSE and DOROTHY HEYWARD

Bess, You Is My Woman - 9 - 1

BIDIN' MY TIME
(from *Girl Crazy*)

Music and Lyrics by
GEORGE GERSHWIN
and IRA GERSHWIN

Bidin' My Time - 3 - 1

Refrain: (leisurely)

BUT NOT FOR ME

(from *Girl Crazy*)

Music and Lyrics by
GEORGE GERSHWIN
and IRA GERSHWIN

Rather slow *(smoothly)*

Refrain:

songs of love,____ but not for me.
on a door,____ but not for me. A luck - y

He'll plan a

star's a - bove,____ but not for me.
two by four,____ but not for me. With love to

I know that

lead the way, I've found more clouds of gray than an - y
love's a game; I'm puz - zled, just the same, was I the

Rus - sian play could guar - an - tee.
moth or flame? I'm all at sea. I was a

It all be -

EMBRACEABLE YOU

(from *Girl Crazy*)

Music and Lyrics by
GEORGE GERSHWIN
and IRA GERSHWIN

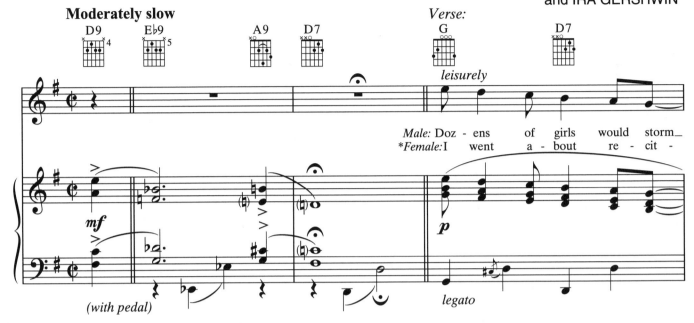

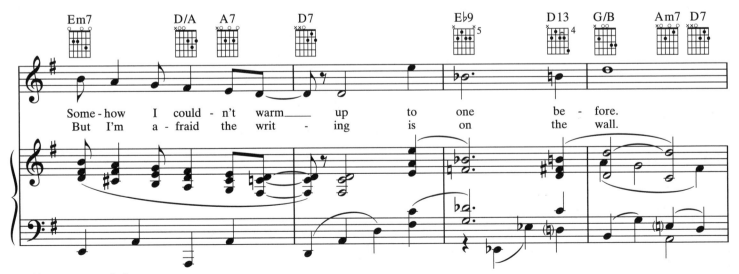

* Alternate verse lyric.

Embraceable You - 4 - 1

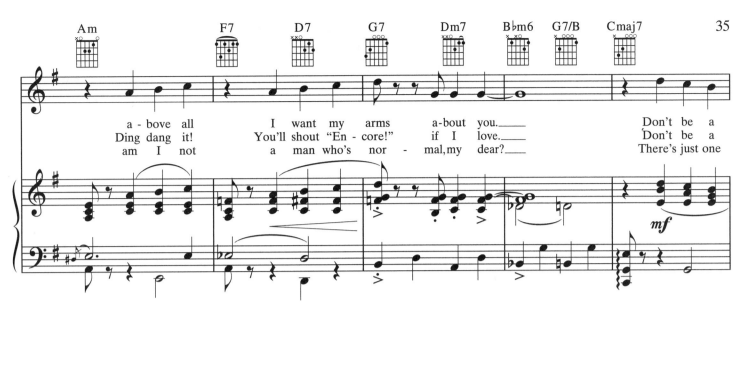

a - bove all I want my arms a-bout you.____ Don't be a
Ding dang it! You'll shout "En - core!" if I love.____ Don't be a
am I not a man who's nor - mal,my dear?____ There's just one

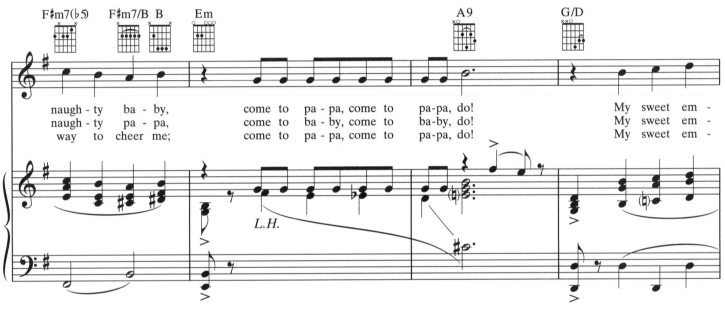

naugh - ty ba - by, come to pa-pa, come to pa-pa, do! My sweet em -
naugh - ty pa - pa, come to ba - by, come to ba-by, do! My sweet em -
way to cheer me; come to pa-pa, come to pa-pa, do! My sweet em -

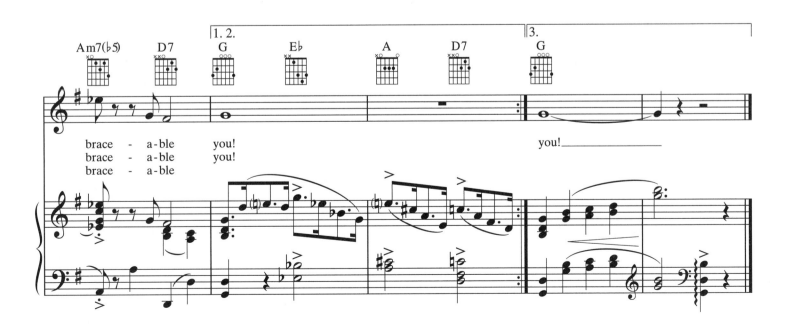

brace - a-ble you! you!____
brace - a-ble you!
brace - a-ble

FASCINATING RHYTHM

(from *Lady, Be Good!*)

Music and Lyrics by
GEORGE GERSHWIN
and IRA GERSHWIN

Got a lit-tle rhy-thm, a rhy-thm, a rhy-thm that pit-a-pats through my

brain.

So darn per-sis-tent, the day is-n't dis-tant

when it-'ll drive me in-sane.

Comes in the morn-ing with-

al-ways shak-ing just like a fliv-ver. Each morn-ing I get up____ with the

sun, (start a hop-ping, nev-er stop-ping,) to find at night, no work____ has been

done. I know that once it did-n't mat-ter, but

now you're do-ing wrong; when you start to pat-ter, I'm so un-hap-py.

A FOGGY DAY (IN LONDON TOWN)

(from *A Damsel in Distress*)

Music and Lyrics by
GEORGE GERSHWIN
and IRA GERSHWIN

Verse:

I was a strang-er in the cit-y._____ Out of town were the peo-ple I knew.

I had that feel-ing of self - pit-y._____ What to do? What to do? What to do? The

A Foggy Day (in London Town) - 4 - 4

FOR YOU, FOR ME, FOR EVERMORE

(from *The Shocking Miss Pilgrim*)

Music and Lyrics by
GEORGE GERSHWIN
and IRA GERSHWIN

For You, For Me, For Evermore - 4 - 1

if we walk on air. All the shad-ows now will

lose us; luck-y stars are ev-'ry-where.

As a hap-py be-ing, here's what I'm for-see-ing: For

poco rit.

Refrain:

you, for me, for ev-er-more._____ It's

p - mf

For You, For Me, For Evermore - 4 - 2

bound to be for ev - er - more._____ It's

plain to see, we found by find - ing each oth - er the

love we wait - ed for._____ I'm

yours, you're mine, and in our hearts_____ the

HOW LONG HAS THIS BEEN GOING ON?

(from *Rosalie*)

Music and Lyrics by
GEORGE GERSHWIN and IRA GERSHWIN

He: As a tot, when I trot - ed in lit - tle vel - vet pant - ies,____
She: 'Neath the stars at ba - zaars of - ten I've had to ca - ress men.____

____ I was kissed by my sis - ters, my cou - sins, and my
Five or ten dol - lars then I'd col - lect from all those

aunt - ies.____ Sad to tell, it was
yes - men.____ Don't be sad, I was must

I CAN'T BE BOTHERED NOW

(from *A Damsel in Distress*)

Music and Lyrics by
GEORGE GERSHWIN
and IRA GERSHWIN

I Can't Be Bothered Now - 5 - 1

I CAN'T GET STARTED

(from Ziegfeld Follies of 1936)

Words by
IRA GERSHWIN

Music by
VERNON DUKE

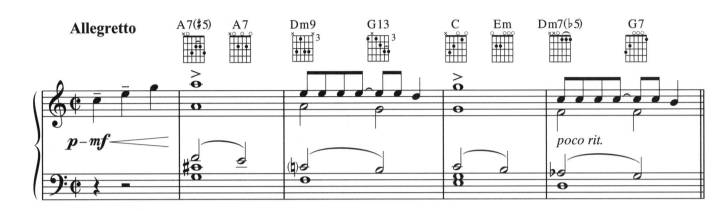

Verse:

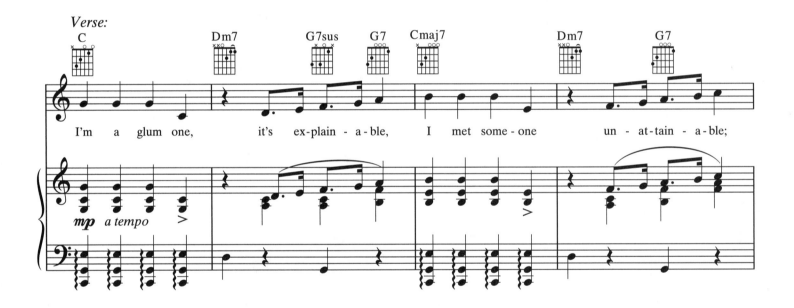

I'm a glum one, it's ex-plain - a-ble, I met some - one un - at-tain - a-ble;

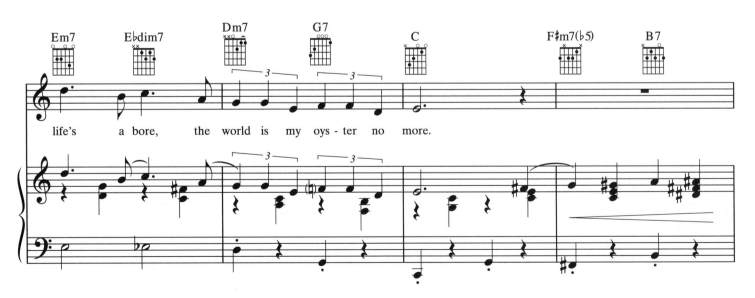

life's a bore, the world is my oys - ter no more.

I Can't Get Started - 4 - 1

I GOT RHYTHM

(from *Girl Crazy*)

Music and Lyrics by
GEORGE GERSHWIN
and IRA GERSHWIN

IT AIN'T NECESSARILY SO

(from *Porgy and Bess*)

Music and Lyrics by
GEORGE GERSHWIN, IRA GERSHWIN
and DuBOSE and DOROTHY HEYWARD

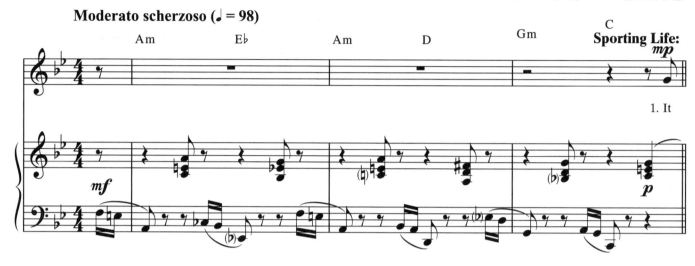

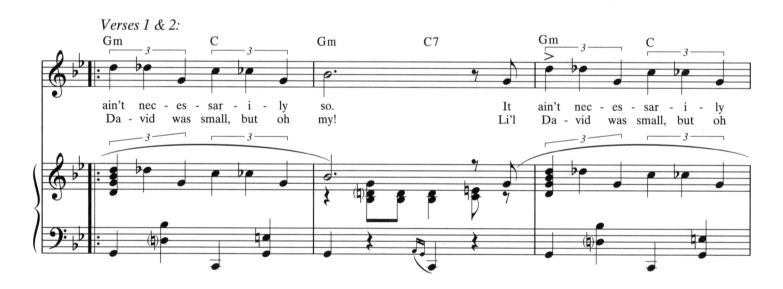

ISN'T IT A PITY?

(from *Pardon My English*)

Music and Lyrics by
GEORGE GERSHWIN
and IRA GERSHWIN

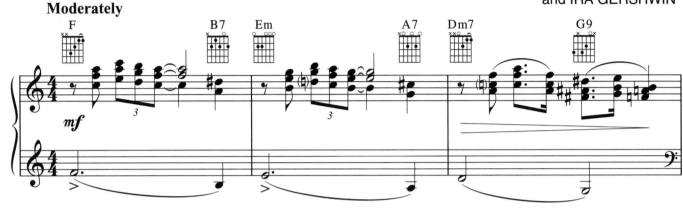

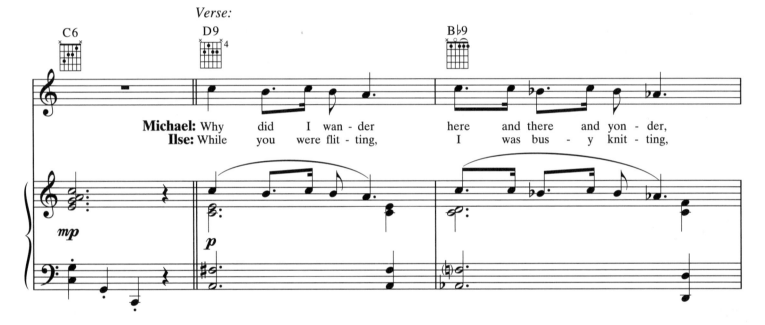

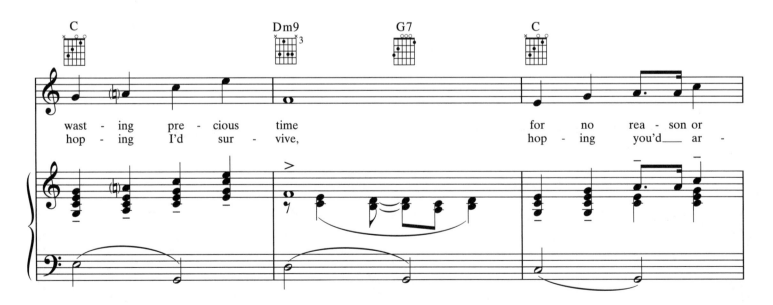

Isn't It a Pity? - 5 - 1

Not fast, with expression

Refrain:

It's a fun-ny thing, I look at you,__ I get a thrill__

con calore

p – mf

I nev-er knew.__ Is-n't it a pit-y we nev-er met__ be-

fore? Here we are at last!

It's like a dream!__ The two of us__ a per-fect team!__

76

Isn't It a Pity? - 5 - 5

IT'S A NEW WORLD

(from *A Star Is Born*)

Words by
IRA GERSHWIN

Music by
HAROLD ARLEN

It's a New World - 5 - 1

Refrain: (with warmth and grandeur)

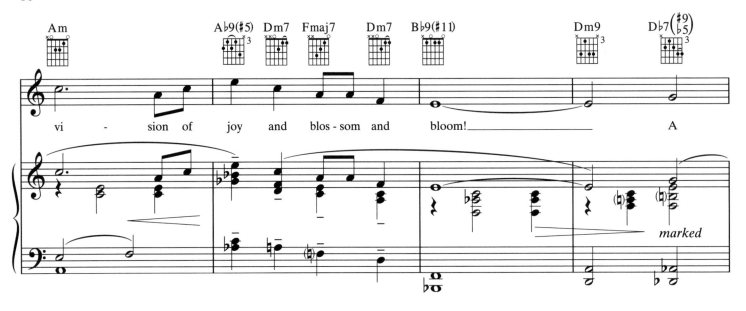

vi - sion of joy and blos - som and bloom!_____ A

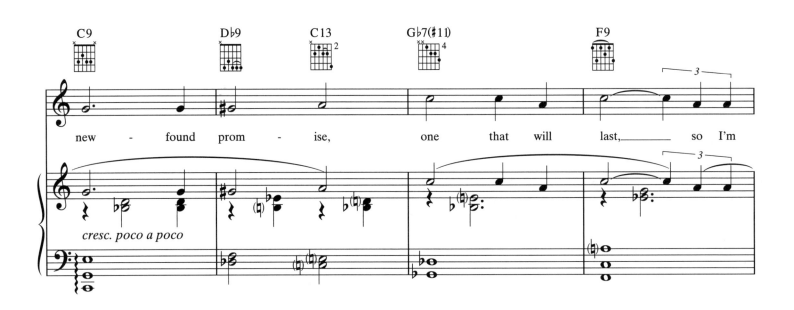

new - found prom - ise, one that will last,_____ so I'm

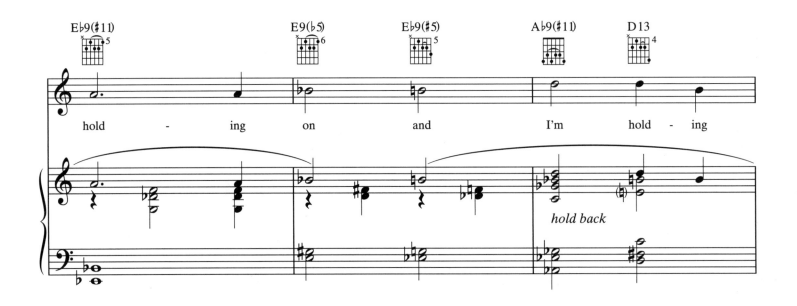

hold - ing on and I'm hold - ing

I'VE GOT A CRUSH ON YOU

(from *Treasure Girl / Strike Up the Band*)

Music and Lyrics by
GEORGE GERSHWIN
and IRA GERSHWIN

Allegretto giocoso

Verse:

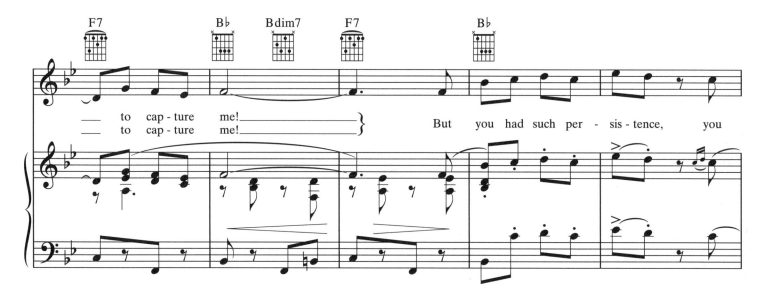

I've Got a Crush on You - 4 - 1

Moderately

LET'S CALL THE WHOLE THING OFF

(from *Shall We Dance*)

Music and Lyrics by
GEORGE GERSHWIN
and IRA GERSHWIN

Things have come to a pret-ty pass,— our ro-mance is grow-ing flat, for you like this and the oth-er———— while

Lyrics:

oh!

If we ev - er part, then that might break my heart! { So, if
                                                     { So, if

you like pa - ja - mas and I like pa - jah - mas,
you go for oys - ters and I go for ers - ters,

I'll wear pa - ja - mas and give up pa - jah - mas.}
I'll or - der oys - ters and can - cel the ers - ters.}

For we know we need each oth - er, so we bet - ter call the call - ing off off.

Let's call the whole thing off! off!

Let's Call the Whole Thing Off - 4 - 4

LIZA
(All the Clouds'll Roll Away)
(from *Show Girl*)

Words by
IRA GERSHWIN and GUS KAHN

Music by
GEORGE GERSHWIN

Liza - 4 - 1

LONG AGO (AND FAR AWAY)

(from *Cover Girl*)

Lyrics by
IRA GERSHWIN

Music by
JEROME KERN

MY SHIP
(from *Lady in the Dark*)

Lyrics by
IRA GERSHWIN

Music by
KURT WEILL

Andantino cantabile

My

Refrain:

ship has sails that are made of silk, the decks are trimmed with gold, and of

jam and spice, there's a par-a-dise in the hold. My

LOVE IS HERE TO STAY

(from *The Goldwyn Follies*)

Music and Lyrics by
GEORGE GERSHWIN
and IRA GERSHWIN

Con anima

The more I read the pa- pers, the less I com- pre-

hend the world and all its ca- pers and how it all will

Love Is Here to Stay - 4 - 1

LOVE WALKED IN

(from *The Goldwyn Follies*)

Music and Lyrics by
GEORGE GERSHWIN
and IRA GERSHWIN

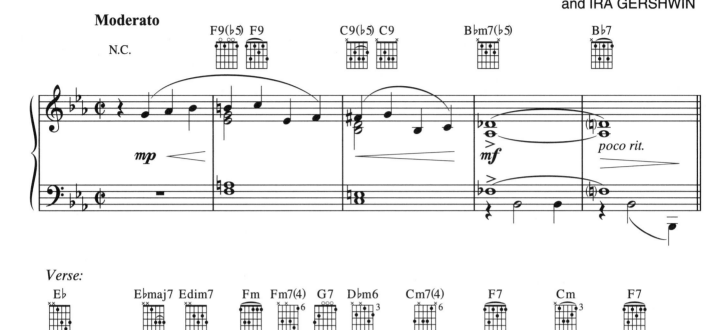

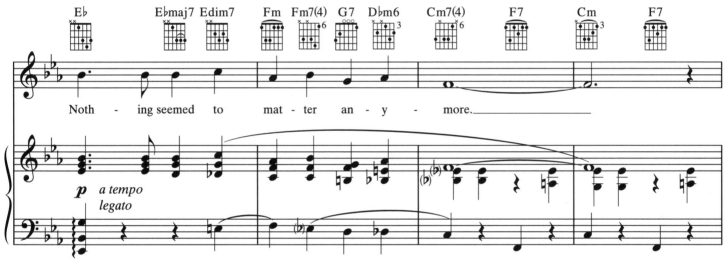

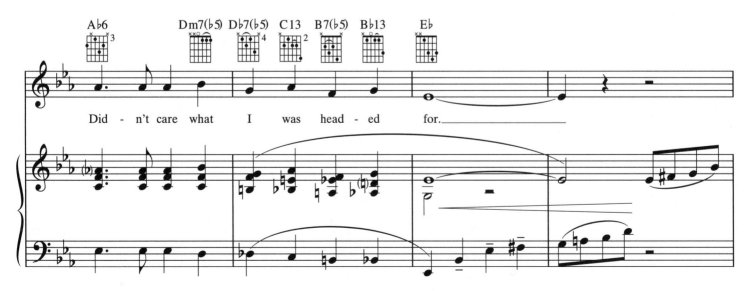

Love Walked In - 4 - 1

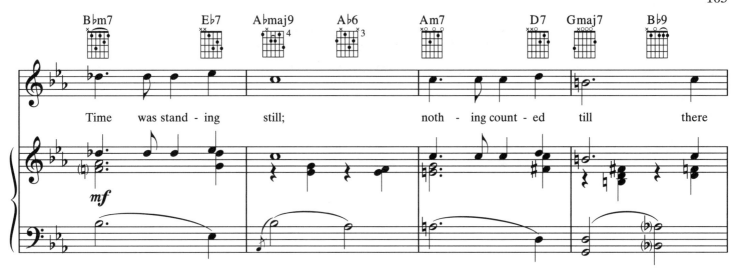

Time was stand - ing still; noth - ing count - ed till there

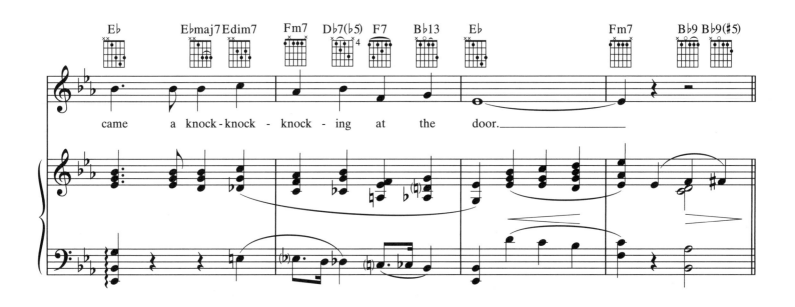

came a knock-knock - knock - ing at the door._____

Slowly, with much expression

Refrain:

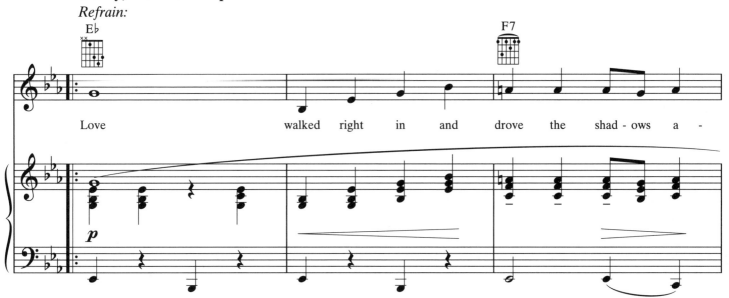

Love walked right in and drove the shad - ows a -

THE MAN THAT GOT AWAY

(from *A Star Is Born*)

Words by
IRA GERSHWIN

Music by
HAROLD ARLEN

The Man That Got Away - 5 - 1

to; but fools_____ will be fools, and where's he gone

to?_____ The road gets rough-er, it's lone - li - er and tough - er, with

hope you burn up, to - mor - row he may turn up. There's just no let-up, the

live - long night and day!_____ Ev - er

OH, LADY BE GOOD

(from *Lady, Be Good!*)

Music and Lyrics by
GEORGE GERSHWIN
and IRA GERSHWIN

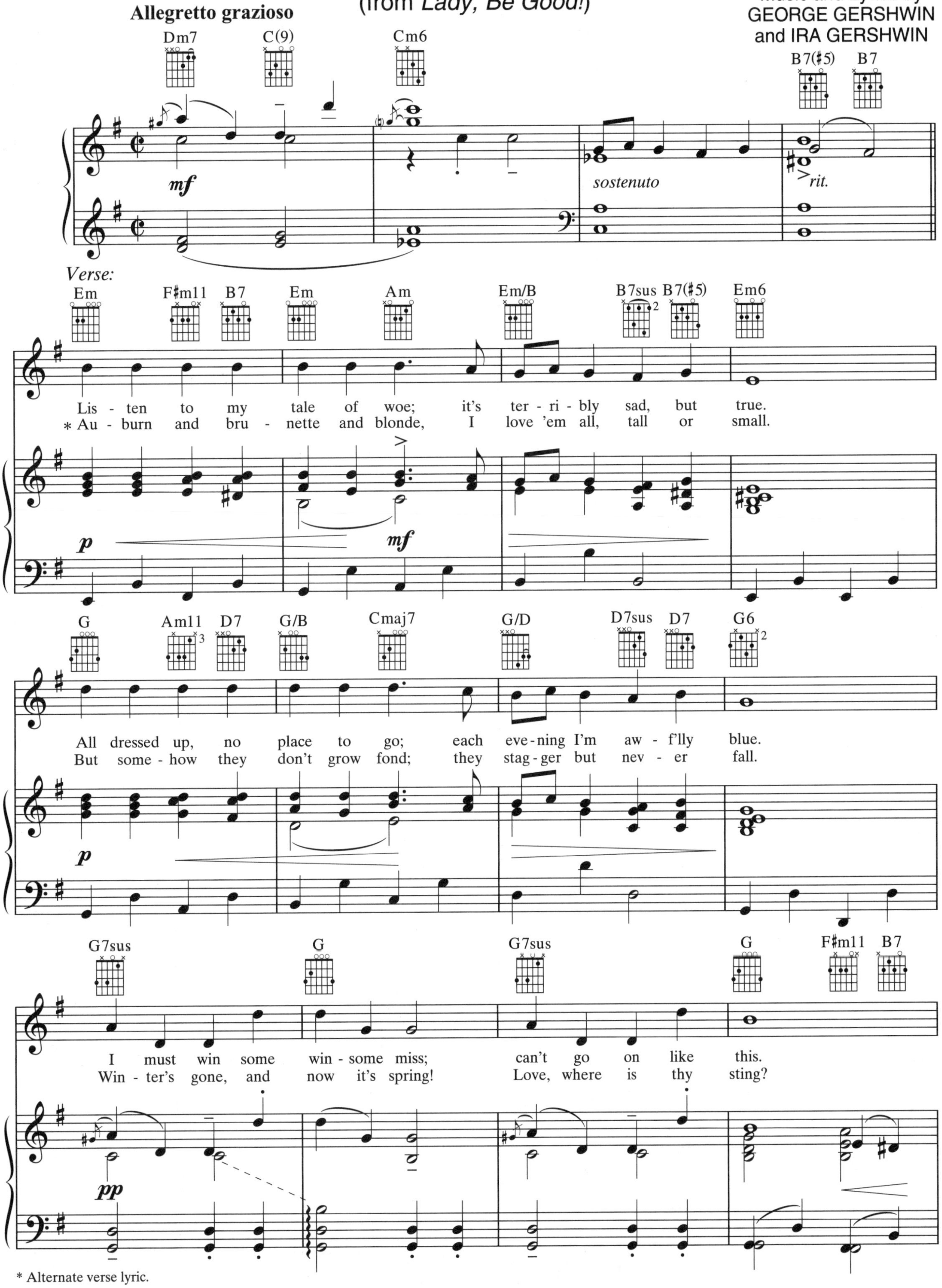

Allegretto grazioso
Dm7 C(9) Cm6 B7(♯5) B7
mf
sostenuto
rit.
Verse:
Em F♯m11 B7 Em Am Em/B B7sus B7(♯5) Em6
Lis - ten to my tale of woe; it's ter - ri - bly sad, but true.
* Au - burn and bru - nette and blonde, I love 'em all, tall or small.
p
mf
G Am11 D7 G/B Cmaj7 G/D D7sus D7 G6
All dressed up, no place to go; each eve - ning I'm aw - f'lly blue.
But some - how they don't grow fond; they stag - ger but nev - er fall.
p
G7sus G G7sus G F♯m11 B7
I must win some win - some miss; can't go on like this.
Win - ter's gone, and now it's spring! Love, where is thy sting?
pp

* Alternate verse lyric.

Slowly and gracefully
Refrain:

THE MAN I LOVE

(from *Lady, Be Good! / Strike Up the Band*)

Music and Lyrics by
GEORGE GERSHWIN
and IRA GERSHWIN

The Man I Love - 4 - 1

Adagio (♩ = 72)
Refrain:

Some day he'll come a - long, the man I love;

and he'll be big and strong, the man I love; and when he comes my way,

I'll do my best to make him stay.

The Man I Love - 4 - 2

LOVE IS SWEEPING THE COUNTRY

(from *Of Thee I Sing*)

Music and Lyrics by
GEORGE GERSHWIN
and IRA GERSHWIN

Refrain:

NICE WORK IF YOU CAN GET IT

(from *A Damsel in Distress*)

Music and Lyrics by
GEORGE GERSHWIN
and IRA GERSHWIN

Verse:

The man who on-ly lives for mak-ing mon-ey lives a life that is-n't nec-es-sar-i-ly sun-ny. Like-wise the man who works for fame, there's no guar-an-tee that time won't e-rase his name.

Nice Work If You Can Get It - 4 - 1

nice work__ if you can get it, and you can get it if you try.___

Stroll - ing with the one girl, sigh - ing sigh af - ter sigh,

nice work__ if you can get it, and you can get it if you try.___

Just im - ag - ine some - one___ wait - ing at the cot - tage door,

PRELUDE I
(ALLEGRO BEN RITMATO E DECISO)

By GEORGE GERSHWIN

RHAPSODY IN BLUE

By GEORGE GERSHWIN

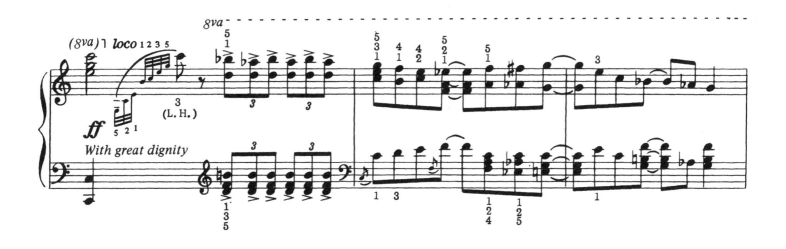

Rhapsody in Blue - 8 - 8

'S WONDERFUL

(from *Funny Face*)

Music and Lyrics by
GEORGE GERSHWIN
and IRA GERSHWIN

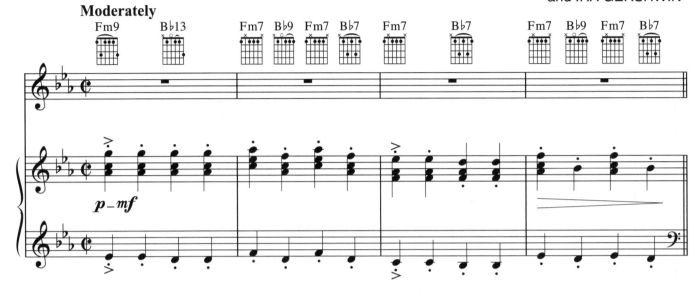

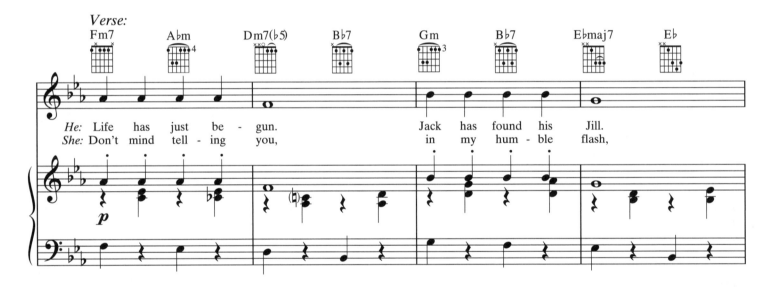

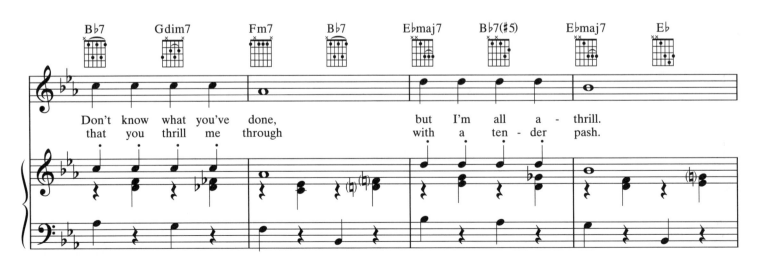

'S Wonderful - 4 - 1

'S Wonderful - 4 - 4

SHALL WE DANCE

(from *Shall We Dance*)

Music and Lyrics by
GEORGE GERSHWIN
and IRA GERSHWIN

Moderately

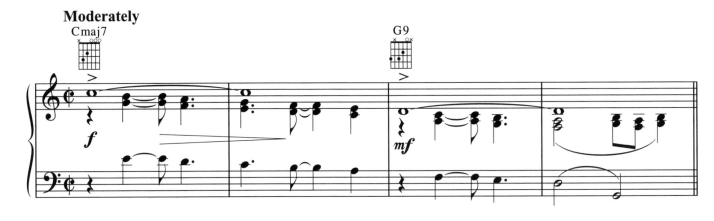

Verse:

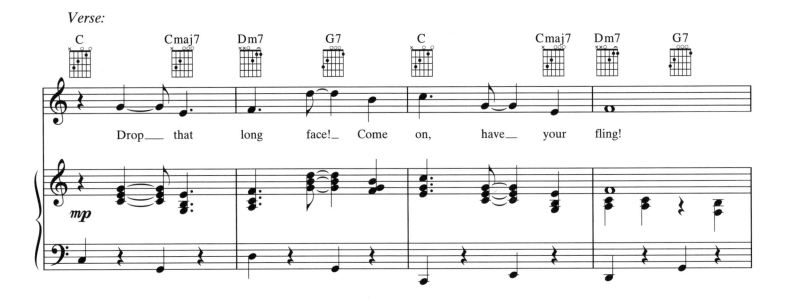

Drop___ that long face!___ Come on, have___ your fling!

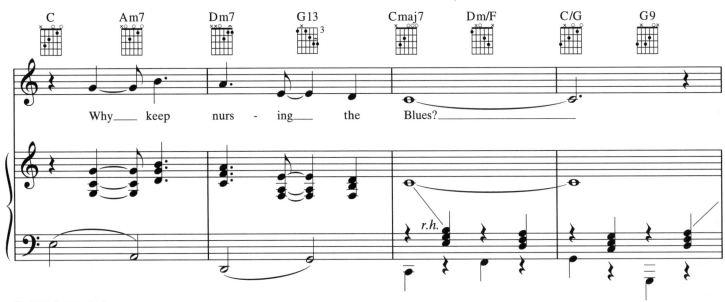

Why___ keep nurs - ing___ the Blues?___

Shall We Dance - 4 - 1

SLAP THAT BASS

(from *Shall We Dance*)

Music and Lyrics by
GEORGE GERSHWIN
and IRA GERSHWIN

STRIKE UP THE BAND

(from *Strike Up the Band*)

Music and Lyrics by
GEORGE GERSHWIN and IRA GERSHWIN

In slow march time

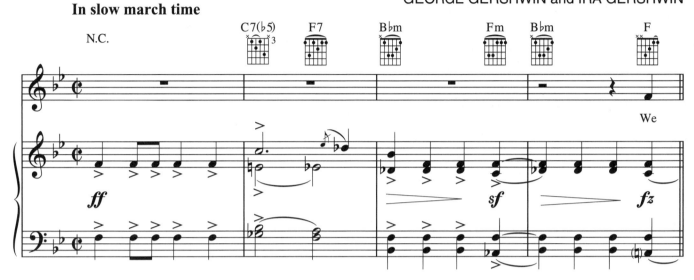

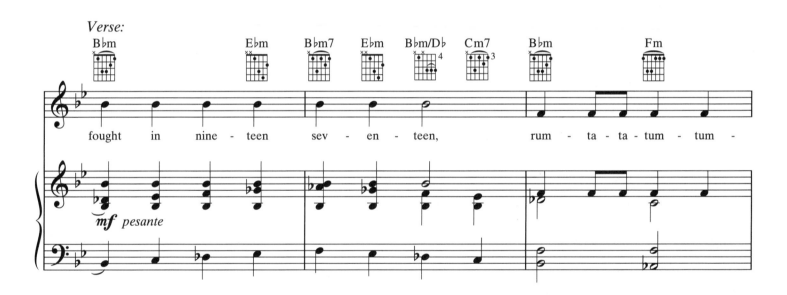

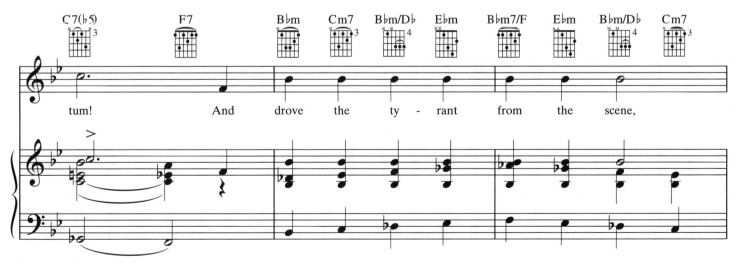

Strike Up the Band - 5 - 1

Refrain:

SOMEONE TO WATCH OVER ME

(from *Oh, Kay!*)

Music and Lyrics by
GEORGE GERSHWIN
and IRA GERSHWIN

There's a say-ing old, says that love is blind. Still we're of-ten told, "Seek and ye shall find."

So, I'm going to seek a cer-tain lad I've had in mind.

Look-ing ev - 'ry-where, have-n't found him yet. He's the big af-fair I can-not for-get.

Someone to Watch Over Me - 4 - 1

(I'LL BUILD A) STAIRWAY TO PARADISE

(from *George White's Scandals of 1922*)

Words by
B.G. DeSYLVA and
IRA GERSHWIN

Music by
GEORGE GERSHWIN

(I'll Build a) Stairway to Paradise - 4 - 1

STIFF UPPER LIP
(from *A Damsel in Distress*)

Music and Lyrics by
GEORGE GERSHWIN
and IRA GERSHWIN

What made good Queen Bess such a great suc - cess?

What made Wel - ling - ton do what he did at Wa - ter - loo?

What makes ev - 'ry En - glish - man a fight - er through and through? It

Stiff Upper Lip - 4 - 1

fight - ing spir - it win?
blight - er say, "What's this?

Quite, quite, quite, quite,
'Ullo, 'ullo, 'ullo, 'ullo,

quite!
'ullo!"

Stiff up - per lip!

Stout fel - la!

When you're in a

stew,

so - ber or blot - to,

this is your mot - to:

Keep mud - dl - ing through!

through!

SOMEBODY LOVES ME

(from *George White's Scandals of 1924*)

Lyrics by
B.G. DeSYLVA and
BALLARD MACDONALD

Music by
GEORGE GERSHWIN

Allegro moderato

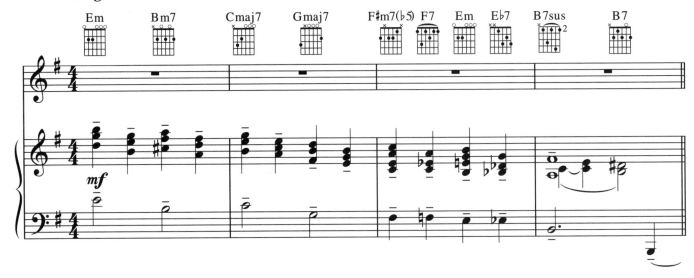

Verse:

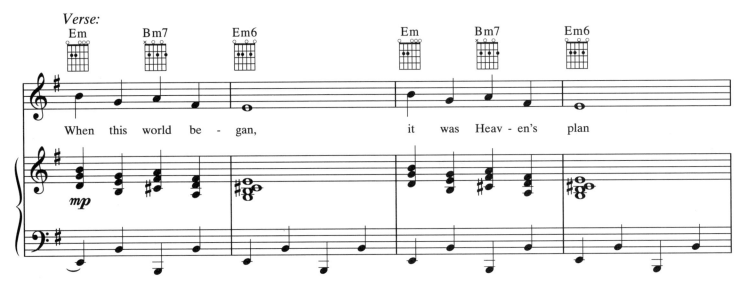

When this world be - gan, it was Heav - en's plan

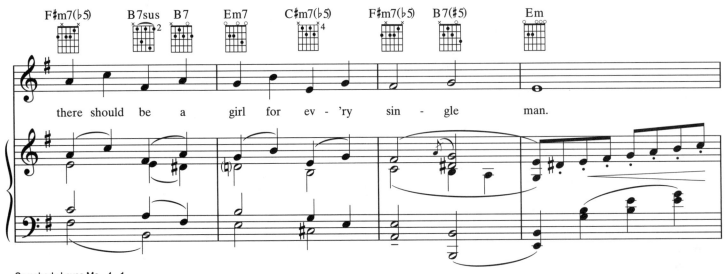

there should be a girl for ev - 'ry sin - gle man.

Somebody Loves Me - 4 - 1

SUMMERTIME

(from *Porgy and Bess*)

Music and Lyrics by
GEORGE GERSHWIN, IRA GERSHWIN
and DuBOSE and DOROTHY HEYWARD

Allegretto semplice

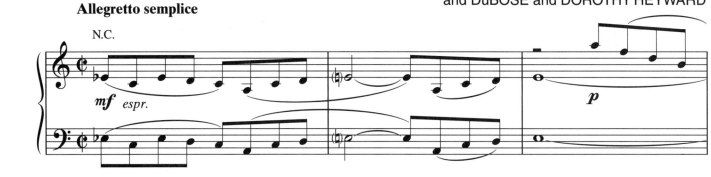

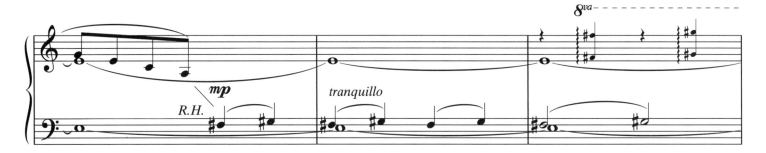

Moderately, with expression (♩ = 40)

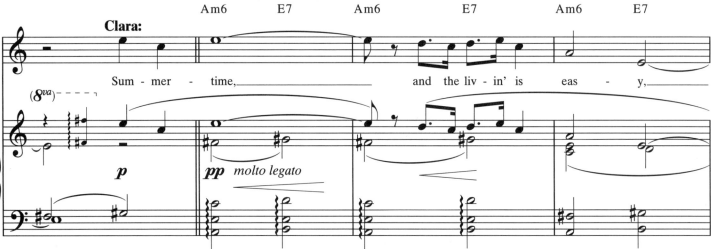

Clara: Sum - mer - time,_____ and the liv - in' is eas - y,_____

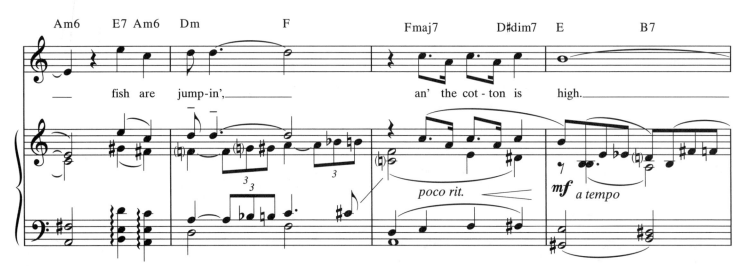

fish are jump - in',_____ an' the cot - ton is high._____

Summertime - 3 - 1

THEY ALL LAUGHED

(from *Shall We Dance*)

Music and Lyrics by
GEORGE GERSHWIN
and IRA GERSHWIN

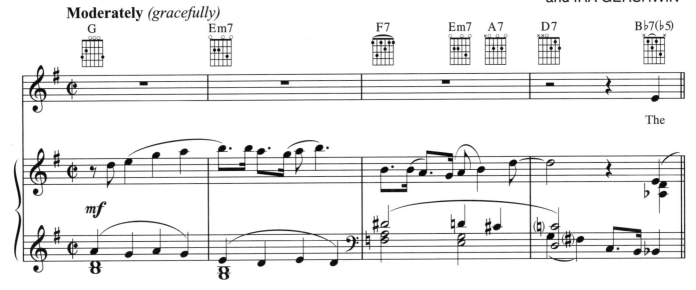

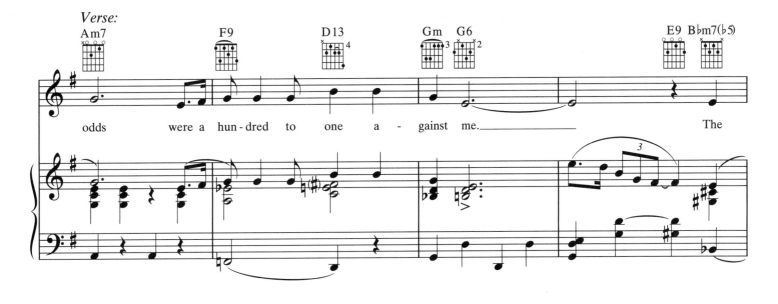

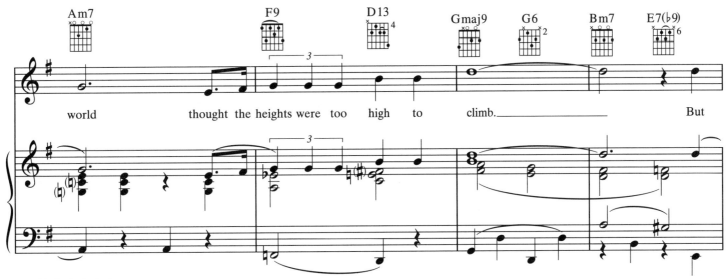

They All Laughed - 5 - 1

SWANEE

(from *Demi Tasse Revue*)

Words by
IRVING CAESAR

Music by
GEORGE GERSHWIN

I've been a-way from you a long time.

I nev-er thought I'd miss you so.

Swanee - 6 - 1

SWEET AND LOW-DOWN

(from *Tip-Toes*)

Music and Lyrics by
GEORGE GERSHWIN
and IRA GERSHWIN

THEY CAN'T TAKE THAT AWAY FROM ME

(from *Shall We Dance*)

Music and Lyrics by
GEORGE GERSHWIN
and IRA GERSHWIN

Verse:

Our ro- mance won't end on a sor- row- ful note, though by to- mor- row you're

gone. The song is end- ed, but as the song- writ- er wrote, the

They Can't Take That Away From Me - 4 - 1

THINGS ARE LOOKING UP

(from *A Damsel in Distress*)

Music and Lyrics by
GEORGE GERSHWIN
and IRA GERSHWIN

Verse:

If I should sud-den-ly start to sing, or stand on my head or an-y-thing, don't think that I've lost my sens-es. It's just that my hap-pi-ness fi-nal-ly com-menc-es. The long, long ag-es of

Things Are Looking Up - 4 - 1

Love's in ses - sion, and my de-pres - sion is un-mis-tak - a - bly through.

Things are look - ing up! It's a great lit - tle world we

live in! Oh, I'm hap - py as a pup since love looked up at

me.

me.

TSCHAIKOWSKY
(AND OTHER RUSSIANS)

(from *Lady in the Dark*)

Lyrics by
IRA GERSHWIN

Music by
KURT WEILL

Allegro barbaro

Ringmaster:

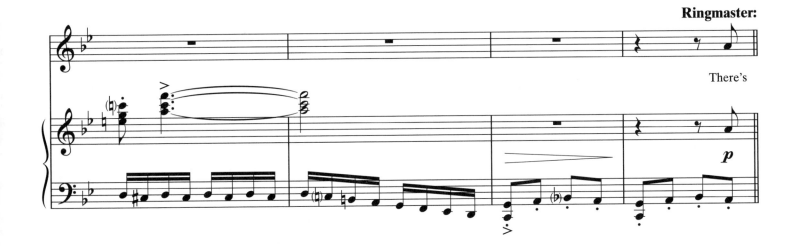

There's

(not too fast and well pronounced)

Ma - li - chev - sky, Ru - bin - stein, A - ren - sky and Tschai - kow - sky, Sa -

Tschaikowsky (And Other Russians) - 5 - 1

Medt - ner, Ba - la - kir - eff, Zo - lo - tar - eff and Kvo - schin - sky, and

Sok - ol - off and Kop - y - loff, Du - kel - sky and Kle - now - sky, and

Shos - ta - ko - vitsch, Bo - ro - dine, Gli - ère and No - wa - kof - ski. There's

Li - ad - off and Kar - gan - off, Mar - ki - e - vitsch, Pant - schen - ko, and

Dar - go - myz - ski, Stcher - bat - cheff, Scri - a - bine, Va - si - len - ko, Stra -

vin - sky, Rim - sky - Kor - sa - koff, Mus - sorg - sky and Gret - cha - ni - noff and

Gla - zou - noff and Cae - sar Cui, Ka - lin - ni - koff, Rach - ma - ni - noff, Stra -

vin - sky and Gret - cha - ni - noff, Rum - shin - sky and Rach - ma - ni - noff. I

WHO CARES?

(from *Of Thee I Sing*)

Music and Lyrics by
GEORGE GERSHWIN
and IRA GERSHWIN

206

stocks and bonds that I've been burned with.

I love you and you love me and that's how it will al - ways be, and

noth - ing else can ev - er mean a thing.

Who cares what the pub - lic chat - ters?